OBSERV

(THEORETICAL AI

ON

MUSKETS, RIFLES,

AND

PROJECTILES.

BY

HENRY WILKINSON, M.R.A.S., M.S.A.,

HONORARY MEMBER OF THE UNITED SERVICE INSTITUTION.

&c., &c., &c.

SECOND EDITION.

1852.

TRAJECTORIES OF DIFFERENT PROJECTILES.

To a Scale of $\frac{1}{5000}$ for distances and $\frac{1}{400}$ for heights.

AAA Improved Model proposed by the Swiss Commissioners in 1850. = "Cylindro - ogivale à deux Cannelures."
BBB Former Dᵒ proposed by Dᵒ in 1848. "Cylindro - ogivale à quatre Cannelures."
CCC Model from Zurich. "Pain de Sucre à une Cannelure."
DDD Ordinary Spherical Bullet.

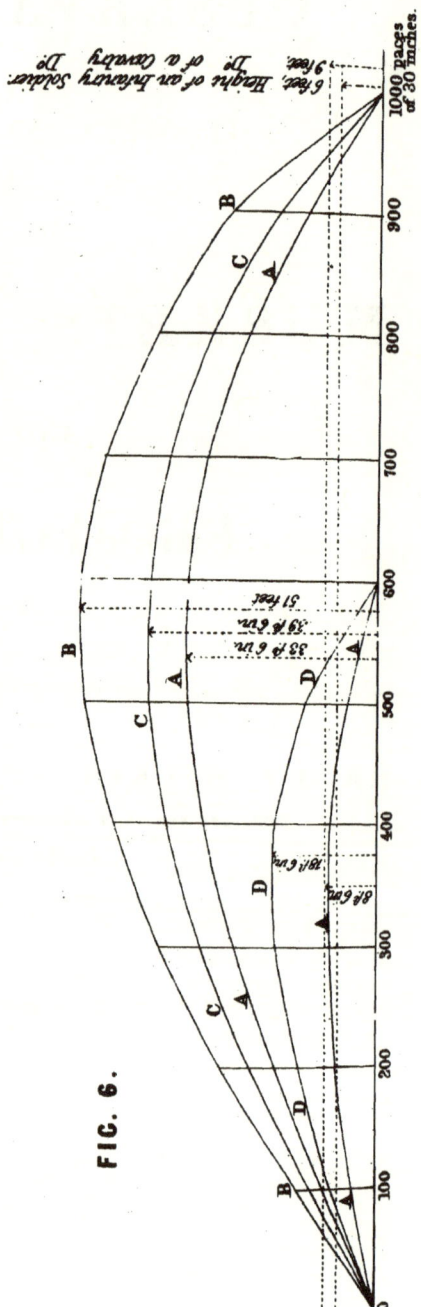

FIG. 6.

Harrison & Sons, litho

THE RIGHT HON. LORD HARDINGE, G.C.B.,

MASTER GENERAL OF THE ORDNANCE.

&c., &c. &c.

MY LORD,

  The great interest your Lordship has taken in all the recent improvements in fire-arms, combined with a perfect theoretical and practical military knowledge of the subject, has caused your Lordship's appointment to the office of Master General to be hailed with universal satisfaction by the nation. I am fully aware of the honour conferred on me by permission to dedicate my second edition to your Lordship, which I attribute more to kindness than to any merit my "Observations" possess; and I take the liberty to repeat what I have before stated, namely, that having for a long time advocated a smaller calibre for our military arms, in consequence of the general adoption in every country of elongated projectiles, which enables us to lighten the soldier's burden by several pounds, and which advantage I feared would be overlooked, I published a small pamphlet last year in order to draw attention to the subject, and I now wish to point out some of the numerous advantages that must result from the general adoption of a much smaller bore than the old musket or than that of the new one proposed for the use of the Minié bullet.

A small bore offers numerous advantages: the barrel can be made much thicker, without too much increasing the weight, and a much longer projectile may be employed, to which a more rapid rotation and greater velocity can be given, without the chance of stripping; in fact, it places the adoption of every improvement that may be made, and every one now existing, in our power; whilst a large calibre renders the use of them, if not impossible, extremely inconvenient.

The advantages of an elongated form of bullet over a spherical one can no longer be disputed; it was demonstrated by Sir Isaac Newton, and Robins recommended it a century ago; the French, Germans, and Swiss have already adopted it, and we at length begin to believe in it.

Now, it is clear that an elongated bullet, to fit the same bore as a spherical one, must be much heavier, yet we are about to perpetuate an enormous error by retaining a large bore, and thus maintain the weight of the old musket, which will for ever deprive us of the power of adopting any and every improvement that may be made in elongated projectiles; for if we suppose two or three diameters to be the proper length for the projectile, its weight, with the present musket bore, will be so great as to render it impossible, from the recoil, to use a sufficient quantity of powder to give full effect and range to the projectile employed. And if the old argument be used that we could employ the ammunition of our enemies, whilst ours being larger, is useless to them, the same argument will equally apply to a *much smaller bore*, for our enemies could make no effective use of our ammunition. Should we adopt a bore of 32 spherical balls to the pound (= 0·56 diameter), our bullet would *drop into* their fire-arms certainly, but the windage would be so great as to render them ineffective; and if it be said that our large balls penetrate further, or do greater damage than the same weight of lead in an elongated form, every one who understands the subject, and has tried the experiment, can prove the reverse is the fact.

By adopting a 32 bore, which carries a spherical bullet weighing exactly half an ounce Avoirdupois, and 0·56 inch in diameter, we adopt a standard known everywhere, and that it is amply large enough I am prepared to prove, as I can fire from *one to three* ounces from a 32 bore; the only limit to the elongation of the bullet being the amount of recoil and the strength and weight of the barrel; and, from the shape of the projectile, its effect is greater than if thrown from a larger bore—so that *wall pieces* might even be made 32 bore. But with respect to the arm for the soldier, 32 bore will give a rifled musket thicker and much stronger than our present musket-barrel, weighing EIGHT *pounds, exclusive of the bayonet,* and throwing a bullet of 500 to 600 grains (or 1¼ ounce), without any unpleasant recoil, and with a charge of powder amply sufficient to produce the maximum effect.

Any bore larger than 32 would make the projectile too heavy; any bore smaller than 32 would greatly increase the expense of the barrel; 32 is the smallest bore that can be obtained at about the same cost as the present musket-barrel, or I would have proposed a still smaller bore, to throw an ounce of lead; and I would also remark, that with a small bore, cartridges can be used with great effect carrying two or three spherical balls to fit the bore, which at 100 yards will separate from one to two feet asunder, and may be employed in the defence of breaches, and on other occasions where it would be impossible, without great recoil and waste of ammunition, to use them from a large bore. The French have used their muskets double-shotted on many occasions when we have probably experienced the effects, without knowing the cause; therefore we ought to avail ourselves of every advantage in our power in case of necessity. I have felt it my duty, knowing our numerical inferiority, to offer these suggestions to your Lordship, convinced that they will meet with the fairest and most impartial consideration.

I have the honour to remain,

With the greatest respect,

Your Lordship's obliged and obedient Servant,

HENRY WILKINSON.

PREFACE

———

THE first edition of this pamphlet having been disposed of in a month, I am enabled in a second edition to explain the principles of a new projectile I have invented, which will, I think, entirely supersede the Carabine à Tige, the Minié, and every other that has preceded it. But I beg it may be distinctly understood as a new system, and not an alteration or adaptation of any one previously existing; therefore it may be properly called "Wilkinson's Projectile," or "Wilkinson's Self-expanding Solid Bullet," and thus avoid the confusion of applying foreign names to an invention, the principle of which not only differs from all others, but is purely English.

OBSERVATIONS ON MUSKETS, RIFLES, PROJECTILES, &c.

Part I.

INTRODUCTION.

"Whatever state shall thoroughly comprehend the nature and advantages of rifled barrel pieces, and, having facilitated and completed their construction, shall introduce into their armies their general use, with a dexterity in the management of them,—they will by this means acquire a superiority which will almost equal anything that has been done at any time by the particular excellence of any one kind of arms; and will, perhaps, fall but little short of the wonderful effects which histories relate to have been formerly produced by the first inventors of fire-arms."

Robins on Gunnery, p. 341.

It is above a century since Benjamin Robins, to whom we are indebted for the first rational work on Gunnery, predicted, in a paper read before the Royal Society, 2nd July, 1747, what is now about to take place; and the truth of his observations becomes every day more apparent.

England, as usual, is the last to adopt any improvement; and after sleeping for a century, has suddenly awakened from a torpid state of indifference to a sense of our insecurity, and a desire to improve the fire-arms of our infantry.

It is therefore of the greatest importance to avoid the adoption of a heavy and inconvenient fire-arm and projectile, when a lighter and better might be substituted. It is only a year or two since it was in contemplation to adopt the Prussian musket, loading at the breech (*Zündnadelgewehr*), the worst of all the bad plans ever submitted for the use of a soldier. And now, without sufficient consideration, the *Minié* musket is to be introduced, 23,000 having been already ordered.

It is perfectly true, that it would be difficult to imagine anything more inefficient than the fire of English musketry at any distance beyond 200 yards. At 500 yards the probability of hitting any one man with a musket-ball is about in the proportion of a farthing to the National Debt. Some very careful experiments were made at Chatham with percussion muskets, in 1846. It may be interesting to state the conclusions arrived at, in general terms, without minutely entering into particulars.

Taking the outside line of the barrel, gives an elevation of about half a degree; and with this elevation the point-blank range is 75 yards, so that at that distance the aim should be taken directly at the object. The deflection even at that distance is considerable; but at 100 yards it is 4 feet 8 inches; at 200 yards, 9 feet 9 inches; at 300 yards, 19 feet! Even at 200 yards, with the musket fixed to a stand, and every scientific arrangement for accuracy of aim, not one ball in ten shots struck a target 11 feet 6 inches high, by 6 feet wide; therefore, beyond 150 yards, the fire of a musket is very uncertain. This great irregularity is mainly to be attributed to the windage and rolling motion of the ball against the sides of the barrel, as well as to the point on which it last impinges on leaving, which varies with every shot.

Then, with respect to range and elevation, the difference between two successive shots at the same degree of elevation, and with the same charge of powder (4½ drachms) amounts to about half the extreme range at long distances; while the lateral deviation is even greater than the difference in the ranges.

To obtain the absolute point-blank range, the musket should be laid with the axis of the bore perfectly horizontal, the range is then to be calculated to where the balls strike the ground from a stand 4 feet 8½ inches high; but the sight along the upper surface of the barrel gives a slight angle of elevation under half a degree, which would give a longer range, but that increase may be set off against the fall of 4 feet 8½ inches, about the height of a man's shoulder.

The following table gives the greatest and least ranges at different degrees of elevation, out of a great number of shots fired at each angle:—

Degree of Elevation.	Range.		Difference between the Greatest and Least.	Observations.
	Greatest.	Least.		
Point blank	218	116	102	The lateral deviations
½°	300	126	174	were greater than these
1°	393	186	207	differences, and many of
1½°	533	261	272	the balls could not be
2°	583	258	325	traced at all.
3°	632	422	210	
3½°	686	408	278	
4°	665	525	140	
5°	797	488	309	

From which it appears that the average ranges with 4½ drachms of powder (since reduced to 4 drachms), the compressed ball weighing 488 grains, diameter, 0·68, diameter of bore, 0·76, windage, without paper, 0·08, are as under :

Average Ranges.		Difference in number of yards for each successive degree of Elevation.
1° elevation	241 yards	
2° ,,	397 ,,	156 A fourth proportion to these numbers
3° ,,	510 ,,	120 is 35; therefore, at 6°, 645 + 35 = 680
4° ,,	599 ,,	89 yards; and at about 9° or 10° the in-
5° ,,	645 ,,	46 crease would be nothing.

By this it appears that no greater ranges can be obtained with a musket by any increase of elevation beyond 8° or 9°; but on the contrary the range will be lessened.

It was found, that in order to strike any object aimed at, the following general rules were necessary, although considered useless beyond 200 yards.

The difference in the thickness of metal at breech and muzzle, giving a slight elevation, at 50 yards, aim 3 inches below the object.

At 75 yards, aim directly at the object,
,, 100   ,,   aim   6 inches above the object,
,, 150   ,,   ,,   2 feet   ,,
,, 200   ,,   ,,   5 feet 6 in. ,,
,, 250   ,,   ,,   11 feet   ,,
,, 300   ,,   ,,   18 feet   ,,
,, 350   ,,   ,,   28 feet 6 in. ,,
,, 400   ,,   ,,   39 feet   ,,
,, 450   ,,   ,,   52 feet 8 in. ,,
,, 500   ,,   ,,   75 feet 3 in. ,,
,, 550   ,,   ,,   95 feet   ,,
,, 600   ,,   ,,   130 feet   ,,

If, however, we turn to page 307 of the Blue Book, we shall find that it was given in evidence before the Select

Committee of the House of Commons on Army and Ordnance Expenditure, May 4, 1849, that the musket, with about 6° of elevation, " would carry 1700 to 1800 yards," that is, *a mile !*

How are such extraordinary discrepancies to be reconciled ? and ought not every officer in Her Majesty's service to know which is correct, or whether it be possible that various muskets can differ to such an enormous extent ?

The musket of the United States does not appear to be any better than our own. Experiments were made at Washington Arsenal in 1843 and 1844 to determine the range and accuracy of their musket, which is smaller than our own, the bore being 0.69 diameter, and the ball 0.64, windage 0.05, the mean weight of ball 397.5 grains, charge of powder 120 grains, initial velocity 1250 feet in a second, as ascertained by the balistic pendulum. The target was 8 feet long by 5 feet high. With about $\frac{1}{4}°$ elevation at 200 yards : of twelve shots, one fell short, one went over, and four missed by lateral deviation, so that only one-half struck the target, although the barrel was securely fixed in a block of wood, and accurately laid 3 feet 6 inches from the axis of the bore to the ground. By reducing the windage to 0.04 instead of 0.05 (which gave 17 balls to the pound instead of 18) and using only 110 grains of powder, the initial velocity was increased to 1550 feet in a second. To attain 500 yards' range, 3° 15' was requisite. See "Report of Experiments on Gunpowder, made at Washington Arsenal in 1843-4, by Captain Mordecai."

If, with all the appliances of scientific knowledge and the coolness of experiment, the results of musketry-fire be as stated, what must be the effect when the smoke and tumult of action be taken into consideration ?

It was stated in the "Times," November 1, 1851, that in one of the recent engagements at the Cape, 80,000 rounds of ball-cartridges had been fired to kill twenty-five men. But this was more than average good shooting, for, according to the French authorities, from 3,000 to 10,000 cartridges were fired, during the last war, for every man killed or wounded, and this also included the fire of the artillery.

There are numerous instances on record equally inefcient, which I have not time to refer to at this moment, but which must be familiar to all military men.

Yet this is the arm with which we have gained our victories, and many persons may consider this fact a sufficient answer to all objections, but is it economy of men or money to waste ammunition when a much better and lighter arm might be substituted, and one half the number of soldiers do greater execution?

This, in my opinion, we are not going to do if we adopt the heavy rifled musket. The elongated bullet afforded an opportunity of reducing the calibre, consequently the weight of the piece, which has been neglected: the new arm proposed, the *Minié* rifle, will have the following *dis*advantages:

1st. Increased difficulty in the manufacture of the balls and cartridges, so that, in foreign countries, where we are *mostly* at war, we cannot make our own ammunition should it be lost, destroyed, or deficient, but must wait for a supply from home. This objection is common to all plans, as we never supply our troops with the means of making their own ammunition, although this might be done, I should think, with advantage.

2nd. The ball weighing *one half* more than the present musket-ball (already the heaviest used by any army in the world); only forty or fifty cartridges can be carried in place of sixty, supposing the burden of the soldier not to be increased, which is surely not intended.

3rd. The arm itself, which is rifled with four grooves, is not lighter, or if lighter, ought not to be so, for the calibre proposed.

4th. The charge of powder (two-and-a-half drachms) is barely sufficient for the weight of the projectile; and if increased, the recoil will be so great as to destroy all steadiness of aim. Greater elevation also must be given, which is objectionable.

5th. There will always be a degree of uncertainty with these projectiles, because the iron cup will not always enter and enlarge the ball equally at every discharge.

6th. The soldier has an entirely new manipulation to perform; he has to bite off his cartridge, and pour in the powder, then to invert it, and put the other end downwards, which in action he will probably forget, and load with the wrong end foremost. This objection has been overruled by stating that the men acquire the habit in a few days' practice.

7th. It cannot be disputed that every hollow projectile must present a larger surface, and offer more resistance to the air, than a solid one of the same weight.

Now the question is, cannot long range and accuracy be obtained by simpler means, with a much lighter arm of equal strength, as great a facility of making the balls as for the old musket, and instead of reducing the number of rounds, to give more, if required, without adding weight to the soldier. This last must be avoided whatever plan be adopted; he is already overloaded, and every pound that can be taken from him is of the utmost importance.

Before entering into any discussion on rifles, it may be advisable to explain what a rifle is. Rifling consists in cutting any number of grooves down the inside of a barrel; it was originally intended to diminish friction, as well as to enable the gun to be discharged more frequently, by forcing the foulness arising from the explosion of the powder, into the grooves or channels cut down the inside of the barrel, which grooves were straight. Another object was to prevent the ball from taking an independent motion of its own after leaving the barrel, which was accomplished to a certain extent, but it was found that straight grooves did not cause the ball to present the same side foremost during its flight, which led to the great improvement of cutting the grooves in a spiral direction, and thus giving to the ball a rotation coincident with its line of flight, and in the direction of the axis of the barrel. This was effected about the year 1600.

The number and depth of the grooves, as well as the turn of the spiral, have varied according to the fancy of the maker, from that period to the present time; but there are certain limits and conditions which must be carefully attended to, in order to produce the desired effect, and from recent experiments, it appears that *the form of the projectile is of more importance than either the number, depth, or turn of the grooves;* which leads us to consider the laws by which the flight of projectiles is governed.

In order to have a clear comprehension of the subject, it is necessary to understand the distinction between the line of sight or aim; the line of fire, or axis of the barrel; and the trajectory, or path of the ball through the air. Each of these three differs considerably, though they are often confounded.

The line of aim is that which passes from the eye along the back and front sights to the object aimed at, as A B C O, Fig. 1. This line is never parallel to the axis of the barrel, or line of fire, in consequence of the metal being thicker at the breech-end than at the muzzle, to which must be added the height of the back sight. These two causes give elevation to the bore, or axis of the barrel, and consequently throw the ball above and through the line of aim at D.

The line of fire is the line E D F, which passes through the axis of the barrel, and is that in which the ball has a tendency to be driven by the force of the powder.

The trajectory, or line of flight, D G O, is that which the ball actually describes in its passage through the atmosphere, from the moment it leaves the barrel until it reaches the earth.

The ball always passes twice through the line of aim, first at a few feet from the muzzle in ascending, at D, and secondly in descending, at O, which is the exact point at which the object aimed at ought to be found, otherwise the aim must be incorrect; and independently of any lateral deviation, the elevation given to the line of fire must be either too much or too little. If the ball pass through the line of aim beyond the object O, then the elevation has been too great, and the back-sight must be lowered. If, on the contrary, the ball cross the line of aim in front, or short of the object, then the elevation has not been sufficient, and the back sight must be raised higher.

The trajectory never coincides with the line of aim or with the line of fire, and hence the great difficulty; for if the ball followed either of these lines, no elevation would be required, as it would be only necessary to hold the rifle steadily in either of these directions, whatever might be the distance of the object. The ball, on leaving the barrel, and under the immediate influence of the line of fire at its initial velocity, continues nearly straight in its flight for a short distance; but the resistance of the air, and the attraction of the earth, or weight of the ball, soon cause it to deviate from the line of fire, and this deviation increases as it proceeds, until it again passes through the line of aim, on its descent to the ground. Thus, the ball never continues in a perfectly straight line for one moment, but always describes a rapidly increasing curve in its passage through the air. To illustrate this by experiment: place three paper screens at ten or twelve yards from each other, and taking aim at the centre of the first, the ball will pass through the three, but on looking through the first hole the second hole will be seen, but not the third, proving that the holes are not in a straight line; the second and third holes will be either above or below the first, according to the distance, and whether the ball was in its ascending or descending curve when it struck the screens.

The force of attraction is constant, and cannot be overcome. Every one knows that a body thrown into the air, and left to itself, falls to the ground by its own weight, or by the force of attraction, otherwise called gravitation. Now the ball, on leaving the barrel, is subject to this force, but being violently propelled by the action of the gunpowder in the direction of the axis of the barrel, it cannot obey either of these forces completely, therefore must yield to their combined influence, which causes it to take an intermediate course in its passage to the earth.

The second force is the atmosphere, which exerts a powerful influence, opposing a constant resistance to the passage of the ball, continually retarding it, until at length it stops it altogether. To many persons it may appear almost incredible that the resistance of an invisible elastic fluid, like the air we breathe, should offer any considerable opposition to the passage of a small ponderous body like a leaden ball, propelled by the enormous force of gunpowder, but such is the fact, as proved by numerous experiments. In 1771 a very careful course of experiments was made at Petersburgh, which proved that, with the same charge of powder, a ball would travel *thirty-four* times the distance it actually does, if it were not for the resistance of the air.

These two forces combined compel the ball to fall to the ground, whatever may be the propelling power, and cause it to describe a curved line, called the *trajectory*. Without these two forces the ball would follow its primitive direction, that is, the line of fire, or axis of the barrel, and it would go on for ever in the same direction, unless it encountered some obstacle to arrest its progress.

If the barrel were made perfectly cylindrical externally, that is, precisely the same diameter at the breech-end as at the muzzle, and the line of aim were taken along the barrel, it would be impossible ever to strike the object aimed at. It follows, therefore, that, if the aim be taken parallel to the axis of the barrel, whatever may be the charge of powder employed, or whatever the distance, the ball will always arrive *below* the object, and so much the more below as the distance is greater, in consequence of the force of attraction and resistance of the air. The idea of a ball ever rising above the line of fire, or the axis of the barrel (as some persons have erroneously supposed it does) is contrary to the laws of nature.

Having seen that the trajectory is a curved line, constantly increasing in curvature, I will endeavour to explain the nature of this curve. In the line A X, Fig. 2, take any distance, A B; the ball will require a certain time to traverse it, during which time it has to encounter the resistance of the air and its own tendency to fall. Consequently it will lose some of the initial force with which it was propelled, and slightly incline downwards towards *b*. If we prolong A *b* by the line *b* C, equal to A B, it will require a longer time to traverse the second space, because it has already lost some of its force in going from A to *b*; and as it requires longer time to pass through the second space, it will be more influenced by the resistance of the air and its own weight, so that it will fall from C to *c*, which is a greater distance than from B to *b*; hence it follows, from the same causes, that at every equal interval of space the ball will fall from D to *d*, a longer line than C to *c*, and so on through the following intervals to *f*.

Thus the trajectory will always continue to describe a constantly increasing curve, until it reaches the earth, consequently the ball never strikes any distant object horizontally, but from above, downwards; and the greater the distance the nearer to perpendicular, though never perfectly so, as the trajectory is always descending or ascending.

Notwithstanding the irregular curved line described by the ball, we are enabled, if the rifle be properly sighted, to reach any object within its range, by elevating the leaf of the sight so as to incline the axis of the barrel more or less above the line of aim, according to the distance, until the second, or descending intersection of the line of aim, exactly corresponds with the place of the object.

This regulation of the sight in the first instance, for various distances, can only be accomplished by numerous trials, and in calm weather, as the direction and force of the wind exercise a powerful influence on the ball, and it requires much experience and judgment to counteract this source of error, which is always variable, and quite distinct from either of the two principal causes already mentioned.

It is quite possible that a man may become a very good rifle-shot by practice alone, without any knowledge of the theory; but no amount of scientific knowledge will make a good rifleman without practice. Even a combination of both will not always succeed; for the first difficulty that presents itself in shooting with a rifle is to maintain a steady aim from the eye, along the line of sight, to the object aimed at, keeping the rifle immovable until the ball has left the barrel, and, if possible, until it has reached the object. This can only be accomplished by holding the breath at the moment of pulling the trigger, and for a second or two after; and as the requisite amount of steadiness is wholly independent of the will, it cannot be accomplished by every one, as it depends on the bodily health, the state of the nerves, and a variety of causes over which one has no control; but it must be admitted that no man can be considered a perfect rifleman, unless he combine practical with scientific knowledge.

It is also essential that he should be a good judge of distances, otherwise it is useless to give him a rifle with elevating sights graduated to 1000 yards, when he may not be able to appreciate the difference between 500 and 1000 yards. The French take great pains to instruct their riflemen in this particular, which we wholly neglect. The little pocket instrument called a *Stadia* is extremely useful for this purpose, and mathematically correct when correctly used. The principles are best explained by a diagram; and by a proper adjustment of the distance from the eye the scale is rendered so extremely simple that a carpenter's rule may be used as a Stadia. For example, if a rule be held 25 inches from the eye of the observer, it will be found that a man (assumed to be 6 feet high from the ground to the top of his hat) occupies exactly one inch when at fifty yards' distance.

$\frac{1}{2}$ an inch at 100 yards.

$\frac{1}{4}$ of an inch at 200 yards,

$\frac{1}{8}$,, ,, 400 yards,

$\frac{1}{16}$,, ,, 800 yards,

and the regular progression at every 50 yards will be thus:

$$\begin{array}{rcl}
100 \text{ yards} &=& \frac{1}{2} \text{ inch,} \\
150 \text{ ,,} &=& \frac{1}{3} \text{ ,,} \\
200 \text{ ,,} &=& \frac{1}{4} \text{ ,,} \\
250 \text{ ,,} &=& \frac{1}{5} \text{ ,,} \\
300 \text{ ,,} &=& \frac{1}{6} \text{ ,,} \\
350 \text{ ,,} &=& \frac{1}{7} \text{ ,,} \\
400 \text{ ,,} &=& \frac{1}{8} \text{ ,,} \\
450 \text{ ,,} &=& \frac{1}{9} \text{ ,,} \\
500 \text{ ,,} &=& \frac{1}{10} \text{ ,,} \\
550 \text{ ,,} &=& \frac{1}{11} \text{ ,,} \\
600 \text{ ,,} &=& \frac{1}{12} \text{ ,,} \\
650 \text{ ,,} &=& \frac{1}{13} \text{ ,,} \\
700 \text{ ,,} &=& \frac{1}{14} \text{ ,,} \\
750 \text{ ,,} &=& \frac{1}{15} \text{ ,,} \\
800 \text{ ,,} &=& \frac{1}{16} \text{ ,,}
\end{array}$$

and so on continually. Now, by reference to the diagram, pl. 3, fig. 7, it will be seen that if E be the eye, ED the distance, and MD the height of the man, and EH the distance from the eye, the line AH will be the apparent height of the man at that distance—for the triangles EDM EHA are both right angled triangles, and have the angle E common to both; they are, therefore, similar triangles, and their corresponding sides will be proportional, therefore ED : EH :: MD : AH and $AH = \frac{MD \times EH}{ED}$. By giving to each their respective values, we have $AH = \frac{72 \times 25 \text{ inches}}{3600 \text{ inches}} = 0.5$, or half an inch exactly. Those who have mastered four books of Euclid will readily comprehend this demonstration. For cavalry, the scale for every distance must be increased one-third, assuming a man on horseback to be 8 feet from the ground to the top of his chaco, which is the average of light cavalry.

Having explained the inefficiency of musketry-fire, described the nature of a rifle, and the laws which influence the flight of the projectile, I will proceed to show what has been done in France and Switzerland on these subjects.

Every experiment proves the decided advantage of the elongated ball over the spherical one for all rifled arms, although the spherical is best for smooth bores. There is no novelty in this idea; Robins suggested it more than a century ago; and Staudenmayer of London, fifty years since, made the bullets for his air-guns cylindro-conical, very nearly the same form as that which recent experiments have determined to be the best. Twenty years since, M. Delvigne, in France, proposed a ball which should be small enough to pass easily down the barrel, and be enlarged by the compression of the ramrod when at the bottom, so as to take the impression of the grooves. This was called the "*balle forcée.*" In 1840, the elongation of the ball was added to this suggestion, and has ever since occupied the attention of military men.

M. Delvigne, in a pamphlet, " *Sur le Fusil rayé, à balle allongée*," thus states the principles of his invention:—

" 1st. To force to the bottom of a rifle a projectile which could be freely introduced at the muzzle, and to enlarge it at the chamber by a stroke of the ramrod.

" 2nd. To substitute an elongated instead of a spherical form, in order to increase the accuracy and the range, by augmenting the weight of the projectile, and thus diminishing the resistance of the air in proportion.

" 3rd. To cause the projectile to expand, either by the force of the ramrod, or by the action of the powder on a hollow in the posterior part of the projectile."

Numerous experiments were tried at Liege and Vincennes, with various modifications of this plan; and it was about to be rejected, when Captain Minié proposed to introduce a small iron cup into the hollow end of the projectile, which being driven forward at the moment of ignition, into the orifice, should expand the lead, and make it take the impression of the grooves in the rifle, though freely introduced at the muzzle, and thus receive the rotation necessary to ensure accuracy of flight.

The originality of this idea rests with *M. Delvigne*, the improvement with *Captain Minié*, but the name of the proposer has become lost in that of the improver, and this arm is now generally denominated *the Minié musket*.

Previously to this, however, *Colonel Thouvenin*, in

1845, suggested the introduction of a piece of iron screwed into the centre of the plug, which he calls the "*tige*," or stem, and which stands up in the barrel sufficiently high to allow the charge of powder to lie freely round it. The bullet being solid, and of a cylindro-conical form, is introduced; the base rests on the top of the *tige* or stem: two smart blows of the ramrod are sufficient to expand it, so as to fill the grooves. This arm is called the "*Carabine à Tige*," and it is used by the "*Chasseurs de Vincennes.*"

See Fig. 3. Reduced section of the bullet, resting on the "tige" or stem in the barrel, and A B the actual sizes of the bullet and stem separately.

The objections to this plan are, the foulness which accumulates round the stem, and its liability to injury; therefore the proposal of Captain Minié has received a greater share of attention, and the Delvigne-Minié system is now about to be adopted in this country; but, in my opinion, however ingenious the contrivance, it possesses the disadvantages I have already pointed out.

Having made many experiments fifteen years since, with balls precisely similar in shape to the Minié, with a conical hole in them, using wooden plugs instead of iron cups, I was fully prepared for the curious results which attended some of my recent trials.

If the hole in the projectile be too large or too cylindrical, the iron cup is forced forward with such violence by the explosion, that it will actually pass through the projectile, leaving behind a cylinder of lead closely fitting the bore of the barrel, and rendering it unfit for service until the breeching has been removed from the barrel, and the lead, which adheres very firmly, has been forced out.

By making the hole rather smaller and more conical,

C

this difficulty may be obviated, as also by giving a small flange or rim to the iron cup; but one singular experiment may be mentioned. In place of the iron cup, I substituted a soft elastic cork fitting the aperture in the projectile very closely, the compression of which I conceived would sufficiently expand the cylindrical part, and make it fill the grooves in the rifle, (which are four wide and shallow grooves, with a spiral of about one turn in seven feet). In some instances it succeeded perfectly, but in many the cork was driven through the lead, carrying off the end, and leaving a long cylinder firmly imbedded in the grooves of the rifle. These experiments were made at Woolwich in September, 1851, in presence of Colonels Dundas and Chalmers of the Royal Artillery, and Captain Lane Fox, of the Grenadier Guards.

Although these difficulties may be surmounted, the objections I have already mentioned remain; and I cannot help thinking that a simpler and better plan might be adopted with less expense, by taking a lesson from the Swiss, as to the reduction of the calibre and the form of the projectile.

By adopting the French system, we should certainly make a great stride in the right direction, namely, by the introduction of rifles and elongated bullets; but by imitating the Swiss we should arrive at once at greater perfection, and be enabled to give a lighter arm, with an equal or greater number of cartridges than our soldiers carry at present.

Experiments have been continued in Switzerland from 1848 to 1851, under the direction of a Commission appointed by the Federal Government, and a new rifle and bullet have been decided on, the principles of which appear to me, much better than any other, calculated for warfare as well as for sporting; by which I do not mean that we should adopt the size and weight of their bullet, but its form and solidity.

In order to render their carabiniers expert in the use of this arm, no other will be allowed in the competition for prizes at their grand shooting-matches.

A very able and scientific report has been prepared in manuscript by Monsieur J. F. Noblet, Major of the Carabiniers of Geneva, who is one of the Commissioners, and also one of their most expert marksmen; and I am indebted to the kindness of Lord Vernon, also a celebrated rifle-shot, for the loan of this manuscript and other papers.

Suffice it to say, that the Federal Government, after numerous experiments for several years, have adopted a rifle weighing 9½ lbs., the bore extremely small, although the bullets, from their elongated form (see fig. 5) weigh 16·5 grammes = 254·249 English grains each, (say 255 grains); their length is 8 lines = $\frac{14}{16}$ of an inch English, and the charge of powder is 4 grammes = 61·624 grains.

One advantage of this size is, that they are enabled to carry 150 rounds of ammunition; and the result of their trials proves that, small as these bullets may appear, they have sufficient force and accuracy to kill a man at 800 yards and upwards. In Fig. 6, I have shown the trajectory of this projectile at different elevations, for 600 and 1000 paces, compared with those of a spherical ball and other projectiles; by which, one very important advantage will be seen, namely, that at 500 yards in the course of its flight, it never ranges higher than 8 feet 6 inches, so as to include both cavalry and infantry; while the spherical ball, to range 500 yards, rises 18 feet 6 inches, consequently can only strike any object at the extreme range in its descent, and therefore is useless at all the intermediate distances when intended to kill at 500 yards.

At 200 military paces of 30 inches each, 20 bullets in succession were put into a target of only 10 inches square.

At 400 paces all the bullets (20) were put into a square of 20 inches.

At 600 paces all (30) were put into a target 45 × 35 inches.

At 800 paces all (40) were put into a target 55 inches square.

At 1000 paces, firing from a rest on a calm day, 100 bullets in succession struck a target 8 feet 6 inches square, and at that distance penetrated three planks of deal placed one inch asunder, and half through a fourth plank, giving 3¼ inches penetration. At this range the extreme height of the trajectory was 33 feet 6 inches, which was considerably less than that of every other projectile tried: the time of flight was also less, being 2⅘ seconds. The form of the bullet, and the number of grooves round the base of it, as well as a proper adjustment of the charge of powder to the turn of the spiral in the barrel, appear to be essential to the accuracy and to the range. It was found that the grooves round the base of the projectile performed the office of feathers, as in an arrow; *one* groove hardly prevented the tendency to turn over in its flight; three grooves retarded its velocity, and consequently diminished its range at the same elevation; two grooves were found by repeated trials to answer the purpose best; although for short ranges the number of grooves appears to be of little importance, as nearly equally good practice was obtained with one, two, three, and four. But at long ranges the difference was very perceptible, and always in favour of two grooves, even when tried from different rifles, in order to ascertain that the difference was not occasioned by the superiority of one rifle over another, but solely by the form of the projectile employed.

The axis of the projectile should always coincide with the axis of the barrel, which cannot be effected so well with a sugar-loaf form, the base of which alone bears on the sides of the barrel; indeed, any form having only one line of bearing round the base, is radically defective; for which reason the cylindrical form is preferable for the posterior part of the projectile; and the grooves round it not only act as feathers, but diminish friction in loading, as well as in firing, while they allow the raised parts of the rifle to enter and impress the projectile more freely. I have used the terms bullet and projectile indiscriminately, as applicable to every form, the term ball being applicable to the spherical form only. The Swiss projectile is represented at Fig. 5, its actual size.

The only objection that can be made to the Swiss method of loading is that more force is required to get the projectile down the barrel, than with the *Minié*, but this is trifling, if the projectile and patch be properly adjusted to the rifle.

There is one peculiarity common both to the French and Swiss systems, namely, the *hollow* or loose charge of powder. In the "*carabine à tige*," the conical projectile, represented at Fig. 3. B, rests on the tige, or stem A, around which the powder lies, and the space is so arranged by the length of the tige, as to be more than sufficient to contain the regulated charge, which consequently cannot be compressed.

In the "*carabine fédérale à balle cylindro-ogivale à deux canelures*," the ramrod has a lump, or projection on it, which prevents it from entering the barrel beyond a certain distance, which is so calculated as to force the projectile down to within a quarter of an inch of the charge of powder, so as not to touch it. The advantage of this plan is, that the powder can never be crushed, or compressed into a solid hard mass in loading; the projectile is always in the same place, and cannot be forced lower, and the fire of the copper cap enters the charge more freely; thus the action of the powder is uniformly the same at every discharge, and uninfluenced by the force employed in loading. It is quite essential (except with my new projectiles) that a greased patch or greased paper should be used with every rifle, as it fills the grooves, and stops all windage, prevents *leading*, and increases both accuracy of flight and range. It is attached to the Swiss projectile in such a manner as to save all trouble of placing it, and is certain to leave the projectile as it quits the barrel, which is important, and cannot be attained when the ball, as in our ordinary military rifles, is stitched into the patch.

After a careful investigation of the various plans proposed, it appears to me that the conditions necessary for a soldier's fire-arm are not fulfilled by the *Delvigne-Minié* system.

The number of rounds given to a soldier should certainly not be diminished, as there are many situations in which 60 have been, and will be, found too few, and the weight should not be increased, being already too great. If it be possible to obtain accuracy of flight and sufficiently long range by simpler means, and with a lighter arm, it would be a great advantage, especially as we have already abandoned the idea of keeping the bullets of all our small-arm ammunition the same size and weight. If the bore of the rifle (for the smooth bore musket must become obsolete in a few years) were reduced to 32, that is, 32 spherical balls to the pound, diameter 0.56, it would carry a cylindro-ogivale projectile fully equal in weight to our present musket-ball of 488 grains, and considerably heavier than the Federal projectile, which weighs only 255 grains, and has been proved to be so effective; indeed, there is a great disadvantage in a ball so heavy as the *Minié* (720 grains originally, but since reduced to 650), as it requires more elevation of the rifle for every distance, and consequently ranges much higher in the air to arrive at the object aimed at, as well as increases the difficulty of the aim. I therefore suggest that experiments should be made with rifles from 32 to 24 bore, but not larger, as by this means a sufficient charge of powder can be given to produce the maximum effect, without too much recoil, and a considerable decrease in the weight of the arm itself, without diminishing the number of rounds of ammunition. At all events it is well worth trying before we adopt too hastily an inconvenient and expensive system, fraught with numerous objections, from which the one I propose is free. However, it is quite certain that whatever may be the nature of the arm employed, that nation which maintains its fleets and armies in the most perfect and efficient state, will not only exercise the greatest economy, but do far more to preserve universal peace than all those mistaken philanthropists, whose tender sympathies are invariably enlisted in the cause of rebels, savages, pirates, and ruffians of every description, without bestowing a thought

on those innocent persons who suffer by their depreda-
tions and murders.

War is an evil much to be deplored, but it ever has
and ever will exist while human nature remains unchanged;
therefore, however paradoxical it may appear, I maintain that whoever increases the powers of destruction is
engaged in the cause of humanity.

Part II.

SINCE the first edition of this pamphlet was published, a considerable change of opinion appears to have taken place, and all parties agree in the necessity of improving our arms and national defences. I hope that the plain statement of facts contained in the preceding pages (published in December, 1851) may have had some influence in drawing attention to a subject of such serious importance, and that the present investigations may result in relieving our soldiers from an useless burden, whatever projectile may be finally adopted. It is much easier to point out defects than to remedy them, but I am now enabled to state that I have discovered an entirely new system, by which I can combine all the advantages of the *Carabine à Tige*, the *Minié*, and the Swiss methods, and avoid their defects; and at the same time reduce the weight of the musket and bayonet from 11 to 8 pounds, while I retain the same length of barrel and the same weight of bullet as that of the old musket, with greater thickness of metal and increased strength of barrel, in consequence of the elongation of the projectile and the reduction of the bore to 32 instead of 11 (or 0.56 diameter, instead of 0.76) as formerly, thus effecting a saving of 3 pounds in the weight of the fire-arm and bayonet only, and about 2 pounds in the weight of the accoutrements, in consequence of the reduction in the size required to carry the 60 rounds of ammunition. It is certain that rifles could never be generally introduced into the army without perfect simplicity of construction and ease in loading; and a rifle is useless unless the bullet be made to enter the grooves and receive the rotation communicated to it by the spiral. All of these conditions are accomplished by means of my "easy-loading, self-expanding, solid bullet," (registered January 22, 1852). The form of it may be expressed more correctly by calling it cylindro-ogivale, with two deep grooves at the base (see fig. 10, plate 3,) and the end-view in a five-grooved rifle.

The term *ogivale* having been lately introduced, and not to be found in many dictionaries, I have given a diagram at plate 3 in order to define it more clearly.

This form appears to be admirably adapted for the anterior part of a projectile, and much superior to the conical or hemispherical, as it throws the centre of gravity more forward than the former, and opposes less resistance to the air than the latter. The ogivale is adopted by the Swiss, and more recently by the French. I have therefore not hesitated to borrow this form for the anterior portion of my projectile, although the posterior part is that on which my new principle depends, and in which its novelty consists, as by means of the two grooves I cause the bullet to rifle itself, although solid, and cast in a mould in the ordinary manner. It enters so freely, whether used in a cartridge or with a greased patch, that a slight pressure of the ramrod is quite sufficient, merely to ascertain that it is down upon the powder, and that it fits tightly enough not to fall out or move forward if the barrel be inverted. There is so little apparent difference in the form of my projectile from that of others, that it may be difficult to comprenend the action; but for illustration: suppose two oranges, placed on each other, to be pressed together, it is evident that by flattening the poles the diameters increase in the contrary direction, and thus resemble the posterior part of my bullet. Again, if a train of railway carriages be at rest, and another train in motion rush upon it, what is the result? The train at rest is not set in motion wholly and driven forward, but the first two or three carriages are smashed to atoms, and the front carriages are hardly moved. This effect takes place with my bullet: the gunpowder, when ignited, is the train in motion—my bullet in the barrel is the train at rest, the hind part, being lighter and having less strength to resist the shock than the fore part, closes up and expands before it can overcome the inertia of the heavier mass of lead in front (which is the cylindro-ogivale portion) and thus expands and fills the grooves of the rifle, so as to stop all windage instantly; and by receiving the impression of the grooves, it acquires the rotation necessary to secure accuracy of flight. Those who have studied the laws of projectiles will readily comprehend these principles; but it may be necessary to explain that the estimated force of gunpowder, at the moment of ignition, is about 2000 pounds pressure on the square inch; or, in other words, 1 cubic inch of gunpowder is instantly converted into about 2000 cubic inches of elastic fluid, which strikes the bullet with a force of about 500 pounds if the area of the base be half an inch, as four square half inches make one square inch, therefore the force is more than sufficient for the purpose required, which is merely to close up and expand the posterior part. However, experimentally, the explosion is found to expand and rifle all the cylindrical portion of the projectile as well as the hinder part, the correct form of which is very essential. Every military engineer knows that a bag of 50 pounds of gunpowder will blow down the strongest double-fortified gates, although nothing but the air be opposed in the opposite direction. The particles of air are driven forward and accumulated on each other so rapidly that the air itself becomes a wall from its condensation, and the gates are blown down. If such be the case, when acting on unconfined air, we may readily conceive that when confined in a tube and acting only on a mass of soft lead, it will drive the weaker parts together before the heavier have time to move out of the way, and thus accomplish the great desideratum of an *" easy-loading, self-expanding, solid bullet,"* never before obtained.

I may observe that the bullet of a rifle should always leave the barrel uninfluenced by the action of patch or paper, for if either be securely attached by tying, or any portion remain in front of the bullet, considerable deflection will ensue. I find, indeed, that much greater accuracy is obtained by merely dipping the base of the bullet, as high as the two rings, in melted grease, and leaving them on a plate till cold—a mixture of hog's-lard four parts, and bees'-wax one part, answer admirably, although any grease will do, and the naked bullet just fitted so as to go down quite easily on to the powder is the best way of loading with my projectile. Let every rifleman remember that grease is indispensable if he desire to fire one hundred or more shots without cleaning. Powder is generally measured, and not weighed, therefore one uniform-sized grain should be used, and *No.* 2 *Percussion* is, perhaps, the best of any. If larger grain be used, the weight should be the same, or the measure be increased in proportion.

Theory in projectiles is useful and important, but it should never be relied on unless confirmed by practice, and I am happy to say that experiment has proved the theory I advance, viz., that a solid projectile can be made to rifle itself and load easily. I am now constructing double and single sporting and military rifles on these principles, with a variety of improvements which will, I think, render them superior to any hitherto made.

So much has recently been said of the "*Chasseurs à pied*," generally called in this country the "*Chasseurs de Vincennes*," that I will close these observations with a very brief outline of their origin. During the investment of Prague by the Austrians, in 1742, John Christian Fischer, with other grooms, having charge of their masters' horses which were turned out to graze in the Isles of Moldau, placed himself at the head of his companions, and repulsed the Austrian hussars, who forded the river with the intention of carrying off the horses. His conduct on this occasion displayed so much judgment and bravery, that he was authorised to organise his little troop, all of them servants like himself. The services rendered by them in 1743 having overcome all prejudices, they took rank in the army, Nov. 1, in that year, under the name of Fischer's Chasseurs, and at the close of the war he had under his command 400 "*Chasseurs à pied*" and 200 "*Chasseurs à cheval.*"

The term "Chasseur" is derived from the Prussians: Frederick the Great raised some free companies to oppose the clouds of irregular troops set in motion by the Queen of Hungary, and as these were originally recruited from the sons of the park and game-keepers of the kingdom, who were strong, active young men, capable of enduring much fatigue, and especially good shots, they

received the name of the " *Bataillons de Chasseurs à pied,*"
which has been retained. These light troops, having been
found of the greatest service on all occasions, have been
continually increased since that period, and at present
amount to about 14,000 men, destined to perform a most
important part in all future warfare. It is said that
every tenth man is capable of hitting a target the size of
a man, at 500 yards, and about every hundredth man can
strike a similar target at 1000 yards. Their drill and
exercises are extremely fatiguing, but well calculated to
make them excellent soldiers ; and they are stimulated by
rewards and honours, as well as allowed an unlimited
number of ball-cartridges for practice, and not restricted
to thirty rounds a year, as our troops are, which is so perfectly ridiculous that no man thinks it worth while to do
more than get rid of them as quickly as possible when
delivered out. Our three regiments of Foot Guards,
composed of the finest men in the world, have thirty
rounds once in three years to make them perfect in ball-
practice, so that many have never fired a ball-cartridge in
their lives; and if these soldiers ever had the misfortune
to meet the Chasseurs, their bravery and charging with
bayonets would little avail, as they are better qualified for
targets than marksmen.

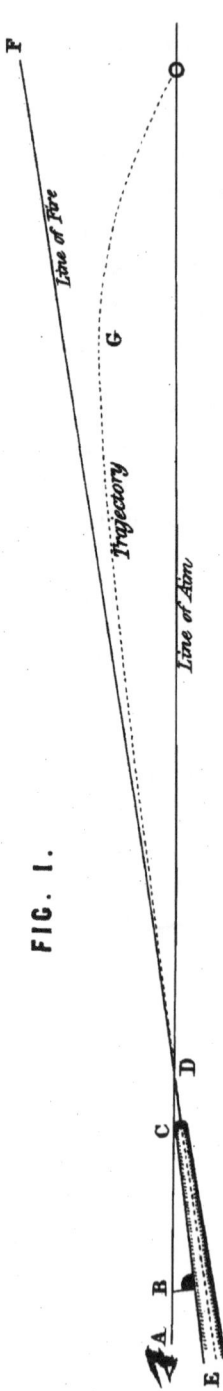

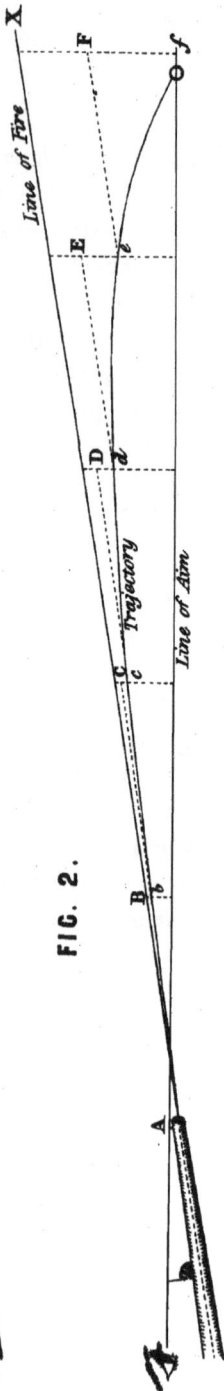

FIG. I.

Line of Fire

Trajectory

G

Line of Aim

P

A

B

C

D

E

FIG. 2.

Line of Fire

Trajectory

Line of Aim

X

F

E

D

C

B

A

f

o

e

d

c

b

a

FIG. 3.

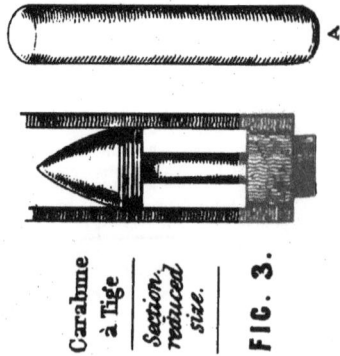

Carabine
à Tige

Section,
reduced
size.

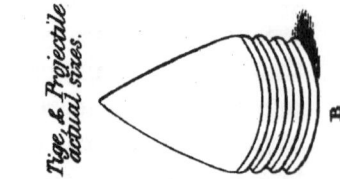

Tige & Projectile,
actual sizes.

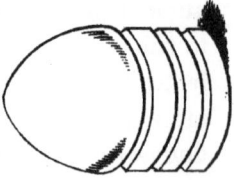

A

B

FIG. 4.

Minié Projectile, & Section
of D.; actual sizes.

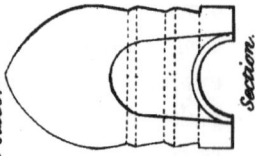

Section.

FIG. 5.

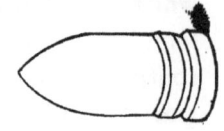

Swiss Projectile with &
without Patch, actual sizes.

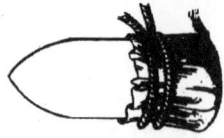

FIG. 7.

Principle of the Stadia

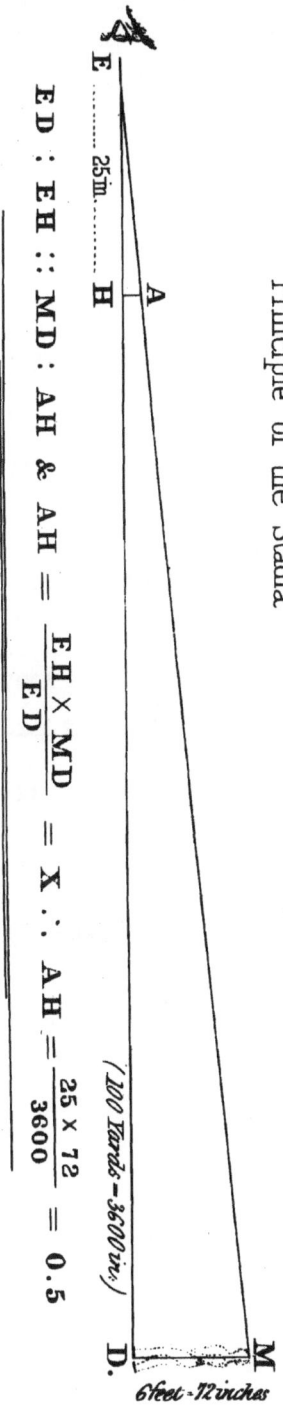

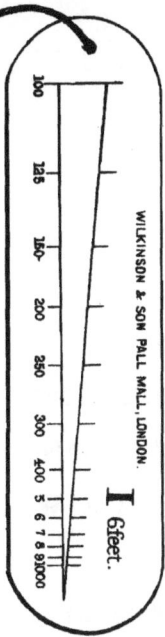

E .... 25in .... H   A

$$ED : EH :: MD : AH \ \& \ AH = \frac{EH \times MD}{ED} = X \ \therefore \ AH = \frac{25 \times 72}{3600} = 0.5$$

(100 Yards = 3600 in.)

6 feet = 72 inches

D.   M

WILKINSON & SON PALL MALL, LONDON.

100   125   150   200   250   300   400   5   6   7   8   9   1000

I 6 feet.

INFY. 8ft   CAVY 8ft
yards   yards

25 inches

FIG. 8.

Triangular
and Vertical
Stadias
reduced sizes.

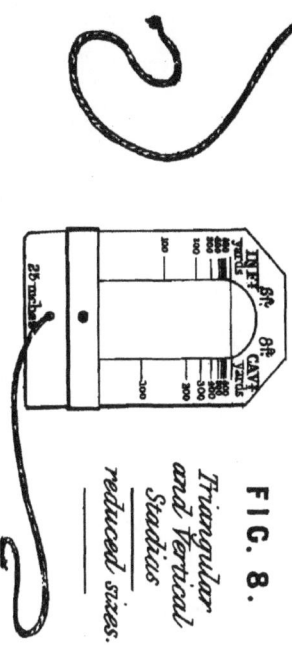

FIG. 9.

Construction
of Wilkinson's
Projectile.

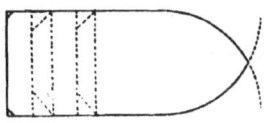

FIG. 10.

Wilkinson's Solid
Self expanding Projectile
with end view of D'ce the bars

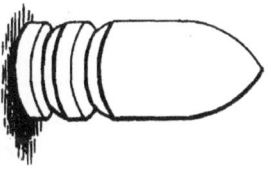

Harrison & Sons, 1

A TREATISE ON THE
ELASTIC CONCAVE WADDING

BY
HENRY WILKINSON, M.R.A.S., M.S.A.

Fig. 1.—Section of a barrel loaded in the usual manner after having been carried a short time.

Fig. 2.—The same after the ignition of the powder.

Fig. 3.—To shew the passage of a single shot if propelled in an angular direction.

Fig. 4.—Section of a barrel loaded with Elastic Concave Wadding, over powder and shot.

Fig. 5.—The same after the ignition of the powder, with the exception of having a flat elastic wadding over shot.

A SHORT

TREATISE

ON THE

Elastic Concave Wadding,

INVENTED BY

J. WILKINSON & SON,

Gun Makers to His Majesty,

TO THE

KING AND PRINCE ROYAL OF PERSIA,

AND TO THE

Honorable the East India Company,

A TREATISE, &c.

—»»❀❀❀««—

TO many persons it may appear immaterial what substance is interposed betwcen the powder and shot in loading; but all experienced sportsmen know that there is a considerable difference in the shooting of the same gun, with the same charge, by merely altering the quality or substance of the Wadding.

The old method of loading with paper is inconvenient, and liable to throw the shot in clusters: the latter objection also applies to cartridges. A great improvement in portability was effected by the introduction of card or paste-board, cut to suit the calibre; but, until the invention of the ELASTIC CONCAVE WADDING, few persons appear to have devoted much attention to the subject.

When it is known that in an ordinary charge (1 oz. ¼) of No. 6 shot there are upwards of 400 pellets, and that at 40 yards the average number thrown into a sheet of paper, 18 inches by 24, does not usually exceed eighty or ninety, it is evident that more than three-fourths of the charge is rendered useless at that distance, and of course a greater proportion as the distance increases.

This circumstance induced us, in 1824-5, to investigate the subject, and to ascertain, if possible, what improvements might be effected by combining a new system of boreing with a change in the nature and form of the Wadding.

After numerous experiments with cork, leather, and other substances, we were enabled to bring to perfection a Wadding which far surpassed our most sanguine expectations.

Before we attempt to demonstrate the advantages of our invention, we will state the defects of card or pasteboard.

Our first proposition is,—*That the common card wadding invariably turns in the barrel, either at the moment of explosion, or immediately after.*

Should this be doubted, we ask if it be possible to imagine that the weight of a loose body, like shot, contained in a cylinder which is always carried in an inclined position, can press equally on every part of a thin card on which it is poured ?

If the pressure be not equal, the moment the powder is ignited, the card A (Fig. 1) must give way on that side which is opposed to the least resistance; and the card B, either from inequality of pressure or friction: *the latter cause* is alone sufficient to prevent the possibility of a card wadding passing along a barrel without turning. A simple experiment will more clearly elucidate this point:—Close a cylindrical glass tube at one end; load it like a gun barrel with card wadding and an ordinary charge; hold the tube in an horizontal position, and slightly agitate it for a few minutes; the shot will assume the position represented in Fig. 1 : or, force air suddenly through an aperture in the lower end of the tube, and the cards will turn.

Admitting that the cards turn, it follows, that a considerable portion of the elastic force of the powder must be lost by escaping through the charge of shot; in the same manner as the power of a steam engine would be decreased by the escape of vapour, if the piston did not fit the cylinder.—See Fig. 2.

The shot, become enveloped in flame, are heated, and in that state give off their lead to

the inside of the barrel much more readily than
when cold. In a double-barrelled gun, the firing
of one barrel several times moves the charge in
the other; so that if it be discharged without the
ramrod having been previously introduced, there
is a probability of injuring the barrel; or, if the
gun be held with the muzzle downwards, the shot
frequently turn the card, and escape.

The corollary to our first proposition is, *that
the shot strike against each other and the inside
of the barrel, forming angles which impede their
velocity.* This must take place if the Wadding
turn, as the impetus given to the shot cannot be
parallel to the axis of the barrel; consequently
angles are formed, and continue to increase, by

the collision of the shot with each other; so that, when liberated from the barrel, many are nearly spent, and fall at short distances, or are dispersed laterally.

To illustrate this, suppose a single shot to be impelled in an angular direction, as in Fig. 3: that angle would be repeated throughout the whole length of the cylinder, and the shot would fly off in the direction represented.

Having thus attempted to explain the disadvantages of the common Wadding, we will endeavour to prove, by Theory and Experiment, that our Elastic Concave Wadding overcomes all the objections stated, and possesses many peculiar advantages.

The first in importance is, The great improvement produced in the shooting, both in strength and closeness.

Secondly; That the gun remains clean much longer, and does not lead.

Thirdly; This Wadding will not ignite, nor can any portion ever remain in the barrel.

Fourthly; The discharge of one barrel does not displace the charge in the other, and therefore every chance of accident is removed.

We have adopted the concave form, in order to place the greatest quantity of powder and shot in the centre of the barrel, and thus invariably oppose the greatest resistance to the strongest impulse, which, combined with the thickness of the edge, prevents the possibility of the Wadding turning, and keeps the shot in a compact cylindrical mass until delivered from the barrel, by which closeness is obtained; and as no portion of the gases generated by the ignition of the powder can escape, the velocity is, consequently, much increased.

This Wadding, being made of wool, is very elastic; and not only wipes the barrel clean every time it is loaded, but, being so slow a conductor of caloric, the heat of the flame does not penetrate to the shot, and the leading is, in a great degree, prevented. An inspection of the Wadding, after firing, will prove this assertion; as it will be found only singed on the side in

contact with the powder, while the upper surface is perfectly white and uninjured.

We invariably use a double Concave Wadding *over the powder*, but a flat and thinner wool-
len one (or even pasteboard) may be substituted
over the shot: pasteboard wadding is, however,
the worst that can be used, unless very soft and
thick, being so liable to turn; we therefore re-
commend the Concave Wadding to be used over
both powder and shot, having found it to produce the greatest effect, and more effectually to
keep the barrel clean. Fig. 4, represents a barrel loaded with our Wadding: Fig 5, the same,
after the ignition of the powder, as contrasted
with Fig. 2.

From a half to one-third of the diameter of the bore is sufficient for the thickness on the edge, *if concave;* but a greater thickness is required to prevent turning, if used flat; and the charge occupies more space in the barrel, not having the hollow on each side to fall into.

The great and increasing demand for this article is the best test of its superiority; and when we state, that it has received the approbation of Lord KENNEDY, Lieut. Col. P. HAWKER, and most of the first-rate sportsmen in the kingdom, by whom it is now used, we conceive we shall do more to render its adoption universal than by any of our own theories or experiments.

Copy of a Letter from Lieut. Col. P. HAWKER.

GENTLEMEN,   Longparish House, Dec. 1st, 1827.

I HAVE tried your " PATENT CONCAVE WADDING" with a large inch and a half gauge Duck-Gun, which, from being on the largest scale, is, of course, the truest criterion to judge of its effects; and I have no hesitation in pronouncing it superior to all other Wadding that I have yet made use of. Indeed, the other kinds of Wadding so decidedly failed, that, until your's was brought out, I found nothing even so good as common oakum.

You are at liberty to make any use you please of this Certificate; and if the other Gun Makers attempt to cry it down, refer them to me.

I am, Gentlemen,

Your's, &c. &c.

To Messrs. J. Wilkinson & Son,   P. HAWKER.
  Ludgate Hill.

The following experiments were made with two double-barrelled Guns, loaded alternately with the Concave Wadding and blue Pasteboard :—

FIRST EXPERIMENT,

With a double-barrelled Gun, 2 ft. 4 in. and 18 bore, at 40 yards distance. Charge of Powder, 2¾ drs.; Shot, 1¼ oz.

Concave Wadding over Powder and Shot.		Pasteboard Wadding over Powder and Shot.		
Order of Firing.	*Number of Shot thrown into a Target 18 by 24.*	*Order of Firing.*	*Number of Shot thrown into a Target 18 by 24.*	*Difference in favor of Con. Wad.*
1 left B¹.	100	3 left B¹.	72	28
2 right	106	4 right	61	45
5 left	97	7 left	67	30
6 right	88	8 right	59	29
9 left	101	11 left	65	36
10 right	87	12 right	69	18
Total	579	Total	393	186

Making an average of *thirty-two* more shot thrown into the space of a sheet of paper, merely by the change of Wadding. Eight sheets of stout brown paper were then folded in four, thus forming thirty-two thicknesses : *eleven shot* were driven through twenty-nine of them when the Concave Wadding was used, and *five* only through twenty-two thicknesses with the Pasteboard.

SECOND EXPERIMENT,

With a double Gun, 2 ft. 8 in. and 14 bore, at 40 yards.
Charge of Powder, 3¼ drs. ; Shot, 1¼ oz.

Concave Wadding over Powder and Shot.		Pasteboard Wadding over Powder and Shot.		
Order of Firing.	Number of Shot thrown into a Target 18 by 24.	Order of Firing.	Number of Shot thrown into a Target 18 by 24.	Difference in favor of Con. Wad.
1 left Bᴵ.	118	3 left Bᴵ.	101	17
2 right	107	4 right	86	21
5 left	123	7 left	91	32
6 right	116	8 right	87	29
9 left	108	11 left	94	14
10 right	105	12 right	89	16
Total	677	Total	548	129
4 shot driven through 36 thicknesses.		1 shot driven through 27 thicknesses.		

Making an average of *twenty-one* more shot thrown into a sheet of paper when the Concave Wadding was used.

FINIS.

JAMES WILKINSON and SON, *most respectfully inform the Nobility and Gentry, that they have lately introduced several considerable improvements, amongst which are*, THE SAFETY STOP, UNIVERSAL RIFLE SIGHT, and PORTABLE REST.

Their STOP *prevents the possibility of any accident arising from carrying both Locks cocked: the construction is so simple, that it cannot be put out of order ; and it may be applied to Guns of any Maker.*

The SIGHT *is capable of the most minute and instantaneous adjustment, by which the accuracy of the aim is considerably increased, and the whole arrangement reduced to scientific principles.*

The PORTABLE REST *forms a seat to fire from in Rifle Shooting.*

9 781445 503448